WHAT OUR FATHERS

NEVER TOLD US!

Struggle Against the Odds

SATO Publications

BY: HALIM A. FLOWERS

ACKNOWLEDGMENTS

To Minkah who gave me LAW

To Muhaymin who have me RELIGION

To George Owens who made me GENERAL

To Ernest Smith who have me VISION

To Tutt who gave me STRATEGY

To Ashanti who have me CULTURE

To Henry Muhammad who showed me
MAN

To Umar who gave me SPIRIT

To my father for what he never told me!

CONTENTS

INTRODUCTION

No boy should be compelled to figure out what it means to really be a man. No boy should have to discover, by his own underdeveloped and immature mind, what process he must go through in order to develop into a mature man. What has been the social result of young boys not having the proper guidance to blossom into growing men?

It is this lack of information that has stagnated the mental, spiritual, and social progression of men today, even though we have made many great strides in technology advancement. A lot of young boys today do not have fathers in their homes nor do they have men in their lives who can show them how to be loving husbands, efficient fathers, and productive men for their families and communities.

Many of us see the negative effects of grown men today. Grown men meaning men who have "grown" and they are no longer "growing" mentally, morally, or socially as men. The high rates of domestic violence, divorces, and single mothers reflects that our young boys are not receiving the proper nourishment to grow into healthy thinking, healthy speaking, and healthy behaving men.

Instead of wasting an entire book on focusing on the problems of our young boys, this book offers sound solutions to teach our young boys how to be successful men. Even though all of the

social ills that plague our young boys
are complicated, the ideas contained in
this brief book provide a simple easy to
implement cure for the daily cancers
that internally destroy our youth.

Halim A. Flowers
05-03-11

MAN?

What is man?
What are the things that make a boy a man?
What is a man made of?

Men are nothing but ideas and energy clothed in flesh and blood, expressed through words, made known through actions. When you look at any man, know that every man has enough energy inside of him to light up an entire city for days because all men are made up of atoms. Atoms consist of subatomic particles which are nothing but energy. Therefore, even though you can physically see a man, in essence, all men are a combination of particles that are nothing but energy.

Everything that you hear a man say, and everything that you see a man do, know that it all comes from his ideas. When you're, hearing and seeing men, you are only listening to and watching ideas. This is all that man is, ideas and energy.

Now, as a man, it is your responsibility to develop your ideas to better the conditions for yourself and the women and children who love and depend on your ability to think and utilize your energy to prosper. When a man fails to develop his ideas, he fails in his position as a man. And, not only does he fail himself and his loved ones, but he also fails the entire planet and everything within it. Man is responsible to secure and sustain all forms of life on this earth.

What is man?
Man is ideas and energy.
What is man's purpose?
To develop his ideas and utilize his life energy to secure and sustain all forms of

life in the earth.
Man Up!

GROWN

The worst thing that you can ever do as a man is to become "grown"! Never allow yourself to reach the mentality that you can no longer grow. To be "grown" is past tense, meaning that you have already grown and are now stagnate or decaying.

A man should always be in a state of growth. Even when the physical body stops growing, a man should be growing mentally, spiritually, and emotionally. Even if you obtain the best college education and go on to teach at the best schools, you always have more to learn about yourself and others. Knowledge is infinite, and so is man in his ability to grow if he truly accepts that he is in desperate need to grow.

If you continue to say, "I'm a grown man!", then you are feeding your ideas and the energy in your body that you can no longer grow. This frequency will resonate and connect with the energy of other people and they will respond in the like manner. You will cut off opportunities to grow as a man, and you will find many doors closed for you that could have been opened had you only changed your ideas towards growth. A rich man never wants to stop growing in his richness, even if he only wants more wealth just to give it away to help others become wealthy.

When people tell you that you are a grown man, correct them immediately, and inform them that you are a "growing man".

CHARACTER

Every man must have good character. However, most boys do not know what character really is and why having good character is very important. What is character?

Character is a combination of all the things that you think, that you speak, and that you do. Everything that a man says comes from what he thinks about the most. In order to have good character, you must make it a habit to think good thoughts. Thinking negative is very easy so you have to pay close attention as to what you are thinking at all times.

What you say is very important to developing your character. People listen to what you say, even when you are not aware that they are listening. The way that you talk often times determines how people treat you. Nobody who has made it a habit of doing good things for themselves and others wants to be closely associated with someone who always talks bad about themselves and others.

The things that you find yourself doing the most is so important because they are what attracts people to you, or repulse them away from you. We all need others to survive in this world, whether it is someone to give you a job or someone to be a customer to support your business. Therefore, as men, it is pertinent that we always do as much good for ourselves and others as we possibly can. Everyone tends to admire a person who treats them good and no one but a bad person would run away from a man who genuinely does much good for others.

Constantly monitor and improve your character. Never trick yourself into believing that your character is perfect!

You always will have room to upgrade the way you think, speak, and act. Do not underestimate the power of great character! Great character can sometimes open doors that money cannot.

TIMING AND CLASS

Recently, Kanye West stated in an interview that he did not think what he had done to Taylor Swift at the MTV awards was wrong. However, he clarified that the timing of his actions was wrong and they did not represent class.

Everything has its time. Flowers do not blossom in the winter and it does not snow blizzards in the summer. As men, we must learn the proper time to think, speak, and do things. Having knowledge is power only when we have .the wisdom to know the proper times to apply what we know.

As a man, examine your daily actions and decide for yourself whether or not they were done at the right time. When you do things out of time, or even speak out of place, then this makes you look immature or foolish, which does not represent class. In order to learn the proper times for things, it is best to study successful people and adapts your ways to the good things that they think, say, and do for a living.

As men, everything you do must represent class. Even if your job is to clean toilets, you should look your best while doing it and be the best toilet cleaner that has ever existed. Everything that you approach in life must be done with class, the most excellent class.

A man should never allow himself to conduct himself with low class. Operating with low class will push away successful people, places, and things that may want to invest in you socially, financially, and spiritually. Furthermore,

do not allow yourself to hang around people who love to display low class because people will believe that they represent your
attitude solely because you affiliate with them.

In a nutshell, do all things in their proper time and place. And, by doing all things the best way, with treating yourself and people the best that is the highest class that you can ever reach. Plus, money cannot buy class!

YOU INCORPORATED

Jay-Z once stated, "I'm not a businessman. I'm a business, man!" As men, we all represent who we are, and we are all selling ourselves to people whether we know it or not. We all need to work for someone, or we all need other people to support our own businesses. Nobody wants to hire or spend their money with a loser.

When we become married, it is business. Our assets become joined with our wives, and our finances become liable as one. We file our taxes as one unit, and if we divorce, our assets have to be divided the same as if a corporation is dissolving. Marriage is a merger of two corporations!

Your character speaks volumes about "You Incorporated." If you are known to conduct yourself with a high level of class and integrity, then people will always want to purchase your stocks and bonds. They are certain that you will continue to increase your worth because your mannerisms and style attracts successful people, places, and things.

As a man, your primary business is developing "You Incorporated." You are your CEO, CFO, COO, President, Board of Directors, and top employee. It is your responsibility to always do what is best to increase the value of your company. Every day that you awake you have to motivate yourself to innovate ways to better promote and advertise your assets to potential investors because no one can invest in a firm that they have never heard of before.

It is important to remember that most top corporations build their worth by their brand name. Microsoft, Nike, Walmart, and Apple all have names that make people want to buy and invest into their products and services because they represent quality and value. People are confident that these companies' products are the best. Therefore, you want consumers to have that same confidence in spending their resources with You, Inc.

Lastly, more products are sold through "word of mouth" (WOM) than by any advertisement strategy. What people think and say about "You, Inc." is very important to the success of "your business". Make sure that your name represents quality and value at all times and people will influence others to invest into "You, Inc." Remember that how you behave in public and private is a direct reflection of your number one business, "YOU INCORPORATED!!!"

MONEY

What is money? Money is nothing but a medium of exchange that we use to purchase products and services. Why is money so important to a man?

We all need money to buy the things that we need to survive, like food, shelter, clothing, and transportation. However, most men complain about not having enough money, o] dream about being rich, but yet they do not know what they want the money for.

As a man, only you can determine why you need money, or how much money you need want to be successful and happy in life. Never believe that money by itself can make you happy. The happiness only lies in the products and services that you enjoy with the money that you obtain and spend.

Furthermore, know that money is not only for spending to consume things. Money has

to be saved and invested as well. A wise man will save a portion of his money to invest into people, places, and things that will generate money. Men must learn to make their money work for them. If you constantly spend all the money that you earn, then you will find yourself always chasing money.

Remember, money is only as important as the things that you want to purchase with it. Focus on what you want in life, then get the money that is necessary to get what you want. Always save and invest!

RICH

What does it mean for a man to be rich? Do you determine a man's worth only by how much money he has compiled and the value of his material assets?

A man is only as rich as the goodness of his health and the amount of intelligence that he possesses. A man can have all the money in the world, but if he is dying from cancer, he is not rich. Another man may not have much money at all, but if he has a billion dollar idea, he will soon have many, material possessions and wealth as long as he has the drive to convert his idea into money.

Never undervalue your health, and never fail to increase your intelligence daily. If you increase your worth as a man, you will soon increase your wealth. People will always recognize the richness of a man's ideas, and they will rush to invest their money into that man. Facebook, Google, Microsoft, all these great companies were nothing but an intellectual property, a mere idea in the minds of men, before they ever materialized into any money. However, you can have the greatest idea ever known to man, but if your health is poor, you will not be alive to reap the benefits of it.

QUALITY AND VALUE

Men must conduct themselves with quality and value at all times. It is important that our very thoughts as men reflect the essence of quality and value. What is quality and value?

Quality is not how much of something that you have but the grade of what you have. A man may have a lot of possessions but if they are all of low quality, then it may be best for him to only have one possession of superior quality. For example, would you rather have a collection of beat down old cars or would you rather have only one Buggati?

In respect of a man, quality is the grade at which you conduct your affairs with yourself first, then others. When you are attending school, you are not concerned with merely completing your task, but you are more focused on how well was the work that you completed. Life is not about just showing up for the championship fight, but it's about winning the title in the best way.

Value is the worth that you place on things in your mind. A lot of times, men confuse the concepts of value and price. For instance, if a pair of shoes cost $100, then that is only the price of that particular product. However, the monetary value of $100 does not reflect the value that each person places upon those shoes. It is not the price of things that determines whether or not you will purchase them most of the times. Rather, it is the value that you place on things that determines whether or not you will decide to obtain them. For example, a person may not be able to afford the price of something that they value, so they will do whatever they have to do, even at the risk of losing their freedom or life, just to enjoy something that they value.

As a man, you must determine your value, and always look to increase it. Only you can determine how much you are worth to yourself and the world.

HYGIENE

A man must keep up his hygiene at all times. Every time that you wake up from sleeping, your first agenda should be to wash your hands. Before you wipe anything out of your eyes or touch your private parts to relieve yourself, you should first clean your hands to prevent spreading germs to your face, mouth, and other parts of your body.

This may sound elementary, but you would be surprised at how many men that I have personally witnessed who neglect their hygiene. I have seen so many men urinate, and fail to wash their hands. Only to put their hands on some food or shake another man's hand shortly thereafter.

As a man, you will have to communicate and network with other people in order to survive and prosper. Nobody wants to speak up close with a man who neglects to brush and floss his teeth. Would you want to shake the hands of someone who does not wash them after he defecates?

Washing and grooming your hair, cleaning and clipping your fingernails, and keeping your mouth clean and fresh is the basis of your physical hygiene. Most importantly, washing your hands constantly. Not only does this prevent you from catching colds, it always keeps you prepared to shake hands with people that you may want to connect with. A genuine smile and a firm handshake are powerful tools in the field of networking. A stranger may infer that because you are clean and smell nice that your social and business dealings with them will be clean and sweet as the cologne that you wear. Never step out of your house and present yourself to the world as a man without having your personal hygiene in order. If you neglect your hygiene, then do not be surprised if the world neglects you.

DESTINATION AND DIRECTION

It's simple, either you already know where you want to go in life and how to get there, or your life is going nowhere! A man must have goals in life, things that he must accomplish, or he will wander in life aimlessly and never accomplishing anything of merit. You cannot be afraid to tell yourself where you want to go in life because you cannot see how you are going to get there. Just tell yourself where you want to go in life then ask other people for directions.

Once you know where you want to go in life, and you are fully committed to getting there, now you must obtain the right directions to your destination. Always seek direction from people who are wise, people that you see to already be successful, and most importantly, people who have already reached your particular destination.

After you have received the best directions, it is your duty to stick to the script. What good is it in having the best map if you refuse to use it properly?

As a man, once you have a destination and direction in life, it is your responsibility to surround yourself with the people, places, and things that are necessary for you to get to where you want to go in the best manner. And, at all cost, you must avoid those people, places, and things that will lead you in a direction opposite of where you are headed.

TIME!

Time is a man's most valuable asset. What a man does with his time in life will determine the value of his living. Knowing that every man is his own corporation, where a man invests his time will determine the wealth or poverty of his business of self.

If you spend most of your time in life watching and playing sports, listening to and watching entertainment, but yet you do not plan on being an athlete or entertainer then
you are wasting most of your life on things that are not of much benefit to your livelihood
and success. Men must invest most of their time into the people, places, and things that
will bring them closer to their goals. Remembering that you are a business, you must never forget that your time is

the greatest wealth that you can ever have. If you are not
utilizing your time into things that will make your company richer, then you can only blame yourself when you are always deep in debt and bankrupt.

A man who loves success is always monitoring his time and taking advantage of it.
The poorest and most miserable men are those who love to waste their time into frivolous
activities that never increases the quality and value of their lives. Use your time wisely!

STRUCTURE

A house cannot stand without a rooted structure. If the foundation is weak then the entire house is fragile and can get blown away by even the weakest of storms. Therefore, as men, we must build our structures on solid ground.

In order to build the structure of "YOU" as a man, you need materials and tools to develop your property. As a man, the main ingredient that you need to fortify your structure is knowledge of who you really are and what do you really want to do with your life. A man must fully know himself, his surroundings, and all of the factors that make up the things that are necessary for him to survive.

When you have a strong structure as a man, your constitution as an individual is powerful, and you cannot be easily broken by adversities. The storms in life are sure to come just as the sunny days. However, a man must be thoroughly grounded into the earth in order to withstand the hardships in life, and to properly handle the successes in life with humility.

ORDER OVER ALL THINGS

Men must have order in all their affairs in life. In life, as men, we will be faced with many ups and downs, highs and lows. However, without order, men cannot properly deal with the challenges in their lives. Furthermore, when a man operates his personal life without order, he will find himself in the habit of always rushing to do a lot of things but never really accomplishing anything significant at all. He will always be "trying" to do things but never seeing things officially done.

Marriages need order, parents need order, homes need order, communities need order, governments and countries need order. Even the planets in outer space operate with order. The affairs of men are no different from the affairs of all other things; all require order.

Whatever it is that you want to accomplish in life, you must have a plan to obtain these things that you desire. A man can have the greatest plan ever but if he does not keep himself in order, he will always deviate from the directions on his map and find himself lost at dead ends or driving off of cliffs.

To establish order, you must set rules for yourself as a man. Then, you have to hold yourself accountable for going against your rules. If society will punish you for breaking their law and order, as a man, why would you not punish yourself for breaking your own law and order?

Once you set goals in your life and put together a realistic plan to reach your aim, as a man, you "must" establish some rules. Reward and punish yourself for going with or against your order. As men, we cannot keep looking for society or the government to establish order in our lives. The government and society are operated and controlled by men just as yourself, so you have to govern yourself as if you are your own independent government.

POWER

A lot of men want to be powerful or in positions of power. However, most men do not know what power is because they have never thought to define it for themselves. What does power mean to you?

As for me, to me, power is the ability to control your thoughts, your words, and your actions. A lot of men are in positions of authority that enables them to dictate what others can or cannot do. However, this is just authority. Power, in my eyes, is when you can tell yourself what to do and what not to do and especially when no one is watching you. To me, that is true power.

By position of family relations or education, a person can be placed in a position to control the movements of others, but yet they cannot muster the internal strength to stop themselves from doing things that they know to be self-destructive. No amount of money, nor schooling can get you the power to control yourself. This is a skill that a man must obtain from disciplining himself. Once you reach this true position of power, the ability to resist your hidden temptations and weakness, then you are in a real position of power to lead others to success.

WORDS

Words are what men utilize to express what they are thinking about. Words are how we
connect with others, which is how we network with other people. It is by words that we legislate laws, make prayers, take vows, and learn about each other.

Even though words are so important to us, most men never devote their lives to learn
and study the words that they use all of their lives. Most people will say that they love you, but yet if you asked them what love means they will go blank. Most men desire power and money, however, they never ask themselves what these two words mean to them as an individual.

The first power that was given to Adam

at the beginning of creation was the ability to name things. Once you have the power to name things, then you control the power to define things. As long as you own the exclusive right to define people, places, and things, then you have the control over how people define their lives and realities.

A man must know and understand clearly every word that he speaks. If not, then he
can never speak with clarity or power. His words can never truly be successful at influencing others to invest into him. It is by words that businesses obtain loans, sell
their stocks and bonds, and market their products and services.

Do your best to learn the origin of words, their meanings, and how to

pronounce them correctly. When a man masters words, he masters his ability to speak to himself and others. He masters the ability to be able to convince others to see his vision and invest in his ideas. All of the great men in history possessed a great command with words, and it was by words that man was created. Learn words religiously, define your own reality, and
tell the world what you demand from it!

LAW

All men have a responsibility to learn about all of the rules, laws, and policies in their city, state, or country that can have a direct effect upon their lives. Men must even have some awareness of international laws and treaties because they can be enforced upon them as well when they are broken. Ignorance of the law is no excuse in a court of law and not knowing about laws will not prevent them from being imposed upon you. A man must protect himself from punishment or he will perish!

First, we must learn how laws are legislated, where they are legislated, and most importantly, why they are legislated. What benefit is it to a man to know all of the rule changes in the NFL or NBA if he is not an athlete but yet he fails to learn the changes in the tax laws that will be taken from his daily earnings?

The importance of learning about law is to protect yourself and your loved ones from being penalized for breaking them. A man cannot do anything within any nation except that it is one way or another governed by some form of law and government agency. If a man remains ignorant about laws then he will always find himself amongst the people, places, and things that are associated with crime, fines, and punishments. This will eventually lead a man to being removed from society or always under the threat of punitive measures, which is not good for a man or his loved ones that depend on him.

Men do not have to become lawyers, but they do have to somewhat comprehend the rules that effect their daily activities.

As a driver, you have to know and adhere to traffic laws. As an entrepreneur who owns and operates your own business, you must become licensed, incorporated, pay taxes, and adhere to the regulations that govern your particular field of commerce and trade. As an entertainer, you have to learn the rules of contracts, copyrights, publishing, touring, and sales.

With information today at the tip of our fingers, invest some of your time into learning the law at websites such as wikipedia, google, bing, and other search engine sites. Every city has its regulations and rules posted online as well. Utilize the resources at your disposal to learn how your life is being governed!

APPEARANCE

Unfortunately, most people tend to judge a book by its cover. Even though you may be a person who looks beneath the surface, you have to think about perception sometimes. Not to say that you always change yourself just to fit in with popular opinion; however, there is a time for everything, and you have to be aware of the proper appearance for each situation that you will encounter in life as a man.

A man does not have to be a fashion guru in order to learn what he should wear at the proper times. Keeping your clothes and shoes neat is the first step to an acceptable appearance. When your clothes and shoes are dirty, even though you may be an intelligent person, most people will perceive you poorly and not feel comfortable being around you. You don't have to wear suits and ties all the time; however, you must wear the best suits and ties for events that is proper for that form of attire. Wearing sweat suits and basketball sneakers to a job interview at a corporation would be improper. The same as wearing a suit and tie on the basketball court.

Keep your clothes clean. Keep your shoes presentable because you are presenting yourself to the world as the CEO and Chairman of the Board of "You Incorporated". When it is time for business affairs, appear in attire fashionable for those affairs. When it is time for relaxation, put on the best fashion for relaxing. All in all, appear to look the best at all times and people will have to respect and treat you the best way.

POSTURE

It is important how a man stands, walks, and sits. Never forget that a man is only ideas and energy. A man that stands with slouched shoulders appears weak in the eyes of others. This is a clear indication that a man is thinking weak and lazy.

When a man stands, his shoulders should be up and wide. This is not done to appear to be macho. This is necessary so that a man can remind himself, and serve notice to the world, that he is fortified by strong thoughts and ideas, and that has he the energy to keep himself straight and upright. A man with bad posture sends signals to all life forms that he is not energetic about life and the living. People are always attracted to a man who appears to be alive and electrified.

Walking with strong posture informs the world that you walk with a purpose. When your posture is correct in your steps, people will recognize that you are traveling towards an important destination, and they will either assist you gladly or get out of your way quickly if they are consumed with foolishness. Walking with good posture shows that you are serious about where you are headband people will respect a man who is serious about his life.

Sitting with bad posture is unhealthy for a man's lower back. Once a man loses the strength in his lower spine, this can negatively affect his entire life. It is difficult for a man to stand, walk, or carry out many tasks once his back is weak. Sit with great posture, if for no other reason than women love men with a strong back.

COMMUNICATION

Communication is the key to success for a man in all the endeavors of his life. In his affairs with God, his parents, his family, his wife, his children, his business affairs, all are dependent upon his ability to communicate. However, most men never were taught that there is a difference between talking and communication.

Communication means to make a connection with a person. Talking is only speaking to someone. Just because you may talk to someone, this does not mean that you have connected with them. In order to connect with people, you have to first understand your audience. The only way you can understand those whom you desire to communicate with, you must first study and learn them. The best way to get to know a person is to listen to them.

Listening is a skill that most men often neglect. This is why most men do hot have healthy relationships and marriages with women. Most men do not listen attentively to understand the person that is speaking to them. Rather, men have a bad habit of only listening to respond. While someone is in the midst of talking, a bad listener is more occupied in their mind with formulating a response to the speaker than attempting to comprehend what the person is trying to convey to them.

It is no coincidence that we have two ears and one tongue. A man should be twice more eager to listen than he is to speak. People, especially women, love men who really show a sincere interest to listen to them. So much so, that some people have a paying career for no other purpose than to listen to patients tell them about their problems.

Learn to listen to understand people and they will assist you when they see that you are paying serious attention to what they say to you. Then, when you decide to speak, speak your words correctly and clearly. Always speak so that you are heard and understood clearly. Never make the assumption that people should understand everything that you tell them. Make it plain!

The ABC's of communication are Accuracy, Brevity, and Clarity. Be accurate and on point about what you say. Never lie or speak about matters that you are unsure of. Only speak about issues that you can command an authority on by citing respected authorities on those subjects. Be brief. Don't overload people. And, always be clear!

DIVERSITY

Once you set your structure solid into the earth, your foundation is strong, and you can now build a house that can withstand the winds. When you build a house, you do not make all rooms with toilets, every room is not a kitchen, nor are all rooms decorated and arranged in the same manner. Therefore, a man is his own temple, and he should be diverse as to how he chooses to build himself up.

When a man attends school, he does not study, one subject alone. When he enrolls into college, the university curriculum mandates that he studies many different subjects outside his particular field of learning. Why is that?

Even though a man may be a lawyer

or a doctor, all of his clients or patients will not only be attorneys and people of the medical field. In any profession in life, a man may have costumers who are of different religious faiths, different cultures, and disparate backgrounds. A man must be diverse in his efforts to prepare himself for the world in order to be able to be successful. The world is globally connected today, so all men must have a global reach in their ideas and manners.

Even though you may love to learn about entertainment, study other things outside of your interest to broaden your reach. This world is about networking to be successful, its all about who you know, and the only way that you can expand your reach is to learn how to reach many people. The only way that you can diversify your network is to be able to make connections with others. This can only be done by studying the basics of different cultures of other people besides your own. Connections are mostly made through casual conversations, and the best way to connect with people from different cultures is to learn about their heroes. When a person recognizes that you have taken out the time to research and speak about the great men and women of their people, they grow to love you as they love their icons.

With that written, let all men make it their duty to study the icons, heroes, and successful men and women from all lands and cultures. To be effective in your diversity, learn well the basic issues that affect all people in all lands. You do not have to master all things, but be abreast of the basics of as many things as you possibly can. If you do not diversify your ideas, you will live within a little box in this big world and close yourself off to many great people, places, and things that can help you become a great man.

NETWORK

Now that you know that all men are only ideas and energy, you should now study how people who think alike connect to each other. Energy has the potential to become electricity, only when it can connect with something else that will make its energy flow. The essence of network is connecting with people that match your ideas and energy.

Look around. Scholars do not hang around fools too often, and criminals do not associate closely with those who do not think about breaking the law. It is thoughts that bring us together or apart. If you want to see where you ideas are at, look no further than the people, places, and things that you surround yourself with the most.. That is a reflection of who you really are and not who you tell people you are.

This world is global today. Everything is about connections. It's all about who you know. You can only go as far as your network. The secret to success is having a master mind group, a strong team, a great supporting cast. No one man can do it all by himself. It takes many talents to build a great nation such as doctors, lawyers, politicians, entertainers, etc. They all serve a purpose in the great order of things. Your network of people, places, and things must be superb in order for you to be a great man.

Never remain in a circle where you are always the smartest person! I am not advising you to neglect those of your network who are not smarter than you, but what I am suggesting is that you always look to surround yourself with people who are smarter than you. This is the only way that you can grow. Constantly look to expand your network and to connect with people who have already accomplished what you want to in life. However, remember that your network starts with your ideas and energy!

IDEAS

Ideas are a man's greatest currency. Let no man who desires riches look nowhere outside of himself, but let him look to his most prominent ideas and see if they are centered in richness. Ideas are what men truly are, what men are made of, and what men will always be.

Men waste their time reading horoscopes in hopes of predicting what the future will bring. Any man who is curious about tomorrow does not have to look at anything besides his thoughts that he thinks the most. This is where the mystery of the next moment resides. In the world of ideas.

As a man, force your ideas to be noble, to be great, and to be what others believe to be impossible. Men, women, and the entire world need you to think miracles. When everyone else thought that it was not possible for man to fly planes, for man to walk on the moon, it was the great ideas of a few men who forced their ideas onto the world of limited thinkers and brought forth the unthinkable. Do not be afraid to think of what you want the most out of life because others cannot see how it can be done. Just think it religiously, and do all that you can to force your ideas on the world. It is due to the "force" of ideas that we have planes, jets, cars, trains, and computers.

In life, the real war is fought in your mind. The battlefield is the land of your ideas. Your ideas are far more valuable than any natural resources such as oil, gold, and other minerals that men continue to fight wars for. Without the treasure of the ideas, man would not know the value in use for oil and other resources. What is oil but liquid mud to the man (mind) that does not know all of the wonderful things that can be accomplished with this black liquid?

It is ideas that see casinos in unknown desert sands in places like Las Vegas. It is ideas that upgraded communication from speaking, to telegrams, to phones, to wireless cellphones, to the smartphones that we have today. It is ideas that combined the computer, camera, video game system, and email all into the smartphone. Ideas rule the world!

Everyday ask yourself, "What have I done with my ideas?". Seeing your mind as far more richer than all banks combined ever, would you allow any person, place, or thing to enter your vault? If not, then pay close attention to the music and television that you allow to share space in your idea world. Ask yourself, "Is this song or movie making my mind richer and stronger, or poorer and weaker?". Remember, your mind is the richest treasure that can ever exist on earth, so be careful who or what you allow into your vault or you may find in life that your mind, body, and spirit are always bankrupt and broke.

Stay close to the people, places, and things that make your keep your ideas more healthy, more stronger, more richer. And, as it is within, so it is without. I think, therefore I AM!

WOMAN

A woman is a man's greatest asset on earth. However, when a man does not understand the purpose and importance of a woman, then he will approach her with a backwards attitude that will always lead to chaotic results.

Women are not recreation for men, nor are they to be treated as our playground. Women were not placed on this earth with men just to be an object to gratify our sexual desires. Women are our partners in governing and sustaining all life forms on this planet. They are our helpers, our teachers, and our source of love and nourishment.

A woman should never be approached for sexual favors unless we commit to them as husbands and life partners. When we enjoy the intimate pleasures of women without marital commitment, we devalue ourselves and lessen their invaluable worth to our planet. When we impregnate our women, it is our duty to always be in their lives during the pregnancy of our children to support them emotionally and spiritually through their nine month challenging birth process. After the birth of our children, our women need us to reside in our homes with them to raise our children upon balanced male/female cultivation. Women need us to show our young boys how to be productive men, husbands, and fathers by remaining in the households with them and fulfilling those three duties in the presence of our children daily.

Women are not our bitches, our hoes, nor are we their pimps. Women are our partners in life, our wives, and the mother of our children. Think of all

women with the sanctity that you
uphold for your own mother.

Made in the USA
Middletown, DE
10 May 2019